PAUL NEWMAN

A Life from Beginning to End

Copyright © 2019 by Hourly History.

Table of Contents

Introduction

He was born on January 26, 1925, in the middle of a snowstorm. It was an abrupt beginning for a man that would make a career perfecting the dramatic entrance. Paul Leonard Newman began his life in the quaint and unsuspecting midwestern auspices of Shaker Heights, Ohio—a suburb of Cleveland. Little did the world know what a megastar had just been born.

Paul Newman was the son of a Jewish father by the name of Arthur Sigmund Newman, Sr. and a Roman Catholic mother named Theresa Fetzko. Arthur was a successful businessman who ran a popular sporting goods store in Cleveland, known as the Newman-Stern Company. The family business paid the bills and allowed for a comfortable and affluent home life. Paul's father naturally thought that his son would one day take over the company after him, but Paul couldn't imagine living such a monotonous and routine life and, from an early age, began to look elsewhere for an outlet for his ambition. At the ripe old age of seven, he thought he had found it when he was cast to play a court jester in a production of *The Travails of Robin Hood* at his grade school. As he stared out at the audience, Newman strangely found himself both elated and terrified at the same time. This was a thrill he certainly wouldn't be able to elicit behind the counter of his father's shop. Paul soon learned to absorb the excitement of the crowd and harness his nervous energy to enrich his performance.

It was a few years after this theatrical debut that his dear mother noted Paul's potential and had him signed up for Curtain Pullers, a special children's outfit run by a local theatrical company called the Cleveland Play House. It was here that Paul would cut his teeth on the basics of showmanship before he was even old enough to run a paper route. Just like that, Newman had charted the course that the rest of his life would follow.

Chapter One

Serving in World War II

"Men experience many passions in a lifetime. One passion drives away the one before it."

—Paul Newman

Newman graduated from his Shaker Heights High School in 1943 before going on to attend college at Ohio University. By his own admission, Newman was a mediocre student at the school and would often joke that he "majored in beer drinking." At any rate, after his first semester came to a close, Paul would have to sober up quick when Uncle Sam came calling. In 1943, the United States was right in the middle of World War II. Newman knew that the possibility of him getting shipped off to combat had existed since he turned 18 years old, and he had already registered and made preparations to join the Navy if it came to that. So it was on June 6, 1943, he was ordered to report to duty.

Initially, Newman was on track to be trained as a navy pilot, a prospect that excited him, but after he failed a physical due to color blindness, he was denied entry. Unable to fly, he was then placed in an Officer Candidate School. This stint didn't last very long either as Newman was small for his age, at barely 100 pounds and 5 foot 3 inches tall (45 kg, 160 cm). Eventually, he was shuffled to a program that had him trained as a radioman and tail gunner for torpedo bombers.

After successfully finishing his training, Newman was sent off to hook up with pilots flying torpedo planes in the Pacific theater. He didn't see much action. According to Newman, his squadron was relegated to some pretty monotonous patrol duty in 1945 when the war with Japan was beginning to come to a close. He would later recollect taking some pot-shots at a few submarines and strafing a few Japanese planes, but beyond that, his day-to-day affairs were fairly sublime. The one time his squadron did get thrown into the fray, Newman was left on the ground because his pilot had developed an ear infection. By a twist of fate, his whole squadron, together with hundreds of other American sailors, were subsequently killed when two kamikaze pilots attacked the aircraft carrier they were stationed on.

Newman returned stateside shortly after the war's conclusion, and upon his return, he went back to college. His education was now fully paid for due to the G.I. Bill, which guaranteed paid tuition for servicemen. This freed him up to be a bit more selective in where he chose to attend. His school of choice this time was Ohio's Kenyon College, where he enrolled in the summer of 1946. Kenyon was a much smaller institution than Ohio University and was also a strictly male school. Newman would later claim that he chose Kenyon for precisely this fact, citing that in the past, he had "become much more interested in the ladies than I was in my studies." Whatever the case may be, it was at Kenyon that he would earn a bachelor's degree in economics and drama.

Another major highlight of Newman's time at Kenyon was his participation in football. Newman was a defensive linebacker, and although he claimed that he was lousy at it, he seemed to truly enjoy his time on the team. With his fellow football players, he was part of a true brotherhood, and he shared the spoils of both fun and folly with his teammates. This included a particularly raucous night on October 23, 1946, when Newman and his buddies were hanging out at the Sunset Club in Mount Vernon, Ohio.

There seems to have been a longstanding rivalry between Newman's team and the local young men, and this rivalry only intensified when local young women were involved. It was apparently at this off-campus party in Vernon that these tensions erupted into a full-scale riot between Newman and his teammates and the townies. Things got so bad that the police were called to put an end to the disturbance.

According to Newman's later recollection, the real problems began when two plainclothes policemen arrived and tried to haul some of the players away. The rabble-rousers apparently did not realize that the men apprehending them were police and tried to fight back. The police managed to pull the two players away from the rest, but a mob of angry Kenyon students gathered on the sidelines, and some of them—Newman included—ended up getting arrested.

In the end, six Kenyon students were hit with the charge of willfully resisting and obstructing a public servant, with all held in jail on a $200 bond. By the time the case went to trial, it quickly became a local circus with over one hundred Kenyon college students showing up to sit in the courtroom. As an indication of how embarrassed the officials at Kenyon College were, every one of those arrested—Newman included—were kicked off the football team and two were expelled. This may seem harsh, but in reality, Newman was lucky that the charges against him were dismissed and he escaped expulsion from the school.

At any rate, now that he was off the football team, Newman began to look for a new social outlet for himself. It wasn't long before he found it in theater. Less than a year after the brawl, he made his way over to Kenyon's speech department to try out for a play they were recruiting for, called *The Front Page*. Newman would eventually be given the leading role for the play, cast as the character Hildy Johnson, and would go on to perform the piece in the fall of 1947. This would then be followed by several more plays, including productions of *Rude Awakening*, *Heartbreak House*, *Antigone*, *The Alchemist*, *Charley's Aunt*, *Ghosts*, and *The Taming of the Shrew*—all performed from Newman's junior to senior year at Kenyon College.

One of Newman's fellow peers from the time would later fondly recall just how well Newman took to the stage at Kenyon. He recalled that Newman "had a wonderful voice that projected through the auditorium with style and grace. It was quite apparent that he had the presence and the charm and the vocal ability. He certainly was more capable than most of the people around."

One of Newman's truly shining moments, however, was when he co-wrote a musical with a fellow student, which they called *The Kenyon Revue*. In this piece, Newman played the role of none other than the school's dean, casting himself as Dean Frank E. Baily. The piece was put together during the spring break of Newman's senior year and in many ways was meant to be his heartfelt sending off of the institution in which he had invested so much of his time. Thinking back on the performance, his fellow co-writer, Doug Downey, would recall, "Paul wrote most of the lyrics, I wrote most of the dialogue, and we shamelessly stole all of the music."

The musical consisted of an all-male cast decked out as chorus girls. The chorus girls followed the dean around as he led the audience on an impromptu tour of a college that jokingly seemed quite similar to Kenyon, without actually saying that the school portrayed was Kenyon. All in all, this great, heartfelt send-off to Newman's alma mater was a stunning success, with the dean himself being one of its biggest fans, stating, "He played me better than I could have played myself!"

Chapter Two

Pursuing His Dreams

"I wasn't driven to acting by any inner compulsion. I was running away from the sporting goods business."

—Paul Newman

Newman finished college at the age of 24, and even though his father would have preferred his son to go into the family business, Newman had other plans. Immediately after graduation, he decided to attend a season of summer stock in Wisconsin's Belfry Theater. For budding actors wanting to break into the mainstream, summer stock was a kind of on-the-job training, in which they were thrust in front of theater-going audiences during summer tours.

Although his father may not have approved, Newman was by now most certainly a self-sufficient and self-serving adult. He had gained a room and board scholarship just prior to his departure, guaranteeing that his way had been paid. So, since it wasn't on his dime that Newman engaged in this enterprise, his father could only grumble that Newman was wasting his time—even if he wasn't wasting his money. From Newman's perspective, pursuing acting made sense at this point in his life—out of the things he had tried his hand in, it was acting that had yielded him the most success thus far. Thus, he ended up at the Belfry Theater.

The theater, located in Wisconsin's touristy Williams Bay, was a place where folks came as far as from Chicago to see interesting and engaging performances for a fraction of the price that they would pay at other more big-name theaters such as Broadway. Newman's first role at the theater was that of a lovelorn enlisted man in a production of Norman Krasna's *John Loves Mary*. After this play came to a close, Newman then began work on a Tennessee Williams piece called *The Glass Menagerie*.

Newman would spend several more weeks performing at the Belfry, and it was during this time that he met an attractive, young actress by the name of Jacqueline Emily Witte. They met on set and fell in love, ultimately getting married on December 27, 1949. Soon enough Jackie, who was a native of Illinois, managed to convince Newman to move to Woodstock with her so that they could work at a local theater company there. The newlyweds initially began life living in cramped quarters that they rented for a monthly fee of $10. Despite the cheapness of their living space, Newman was really struggling to make a living at this point, and upon learning that his wife was pregnant, he began to really scramble for a way to make more money. In his desperation, he even briefly worked as a farmhand on a property owned by his landlord.

It was in the spring of 1950, while he was laboring to eke out an existence with Jackie in Illinois, that Paul received the news that his father's health had taken a turn for the worse. Overwhelmed by a sudden sense of obligation and duty, Paul and Jackie packed up and moved to Shaker Heights, Ohio, so that they could be of assistance. Newman planned on the move being a temporary one, hoping to help out at the family store until his father recovered from his illness. Sadly, there would be no recovery, and Newman's father, Arthur, would pass away just a few weeks after he arrived.

Not only was Paul grieved to hear of the loss of his father, but he was also deeply saddened and troubled by the knowledge of what his death might mean. Newman knew full well that the loss of the family patriarch meant that it was upon his shoulders that the family business would fall next. This, of course, would mean that he would have to forget all about his budding acting career in favor of running ground operations for the Newman-Stern Company in Cleveland.

After his father's funeral, weighed down by the obligation and expectations foisted upon him, he began to work in tandem with his brother Art and his uncle Joe at the family business. In the meantime, he and Jackie moved into a modest rental in Bedford, situated on the edge of Cleveland. It was right around this time, on September 23, 1950, that Newman's first child—a little boy subsequently named Alan Scott—was born. Despite his misgivings with taking over the family business, Paul Newman did his best over the next few months to make his father proud. Yet he couldn't help but feel resentful.

He had left home to get away from the predictable nine-to-five workday of his father, and here he was being sucked right back into it. The gravity of the situation he was thrust into began to weigh heavily on him, and finally, unable to take it anymore, he marched into his brother's office and informed him that he wanted to leave the company. Newman then proceeded to plead with his mystified brother to take the burden off of his shoulders by taking sole ownership of the company. But Art had other plans as well, and he quickly determined that if his brother Paul was not going to be a part of the family business, then neither was he.

As such, it then fell upon uncle Joe to figure out what to do with it all. Unbeknownst to Paul, Joe had already been vigorously shopping around for someone to buy the company in order to take it off their hands for good. He was eventually able to sell it to the local retail juggernaut of Marcus Department Stores. With the family business now someone else's responsibility, Newman was once again free to pursue his dreams.

Chapter Three

Early Career in TV

"To be an actor, you have to be a child."

—Paul Newman

Paul Newman, newly emancipated from his father's former business, took his share of the sale and went off to New Haven, Connecticut. Why New Haven? Paul determined that he was going to go back to school—Yale University no less—to get a master's degree in fine arts. Here he, Jackie, and their young son boarded at an old rental house turned into an apartment. Their section of the unit was on the upper floor, and their creaky floor was two other families' ceiling down below. It was a precarious living situation for the young couple, but for the then 26-year-old Newman, it was well worth it if he was allowed to follow his heart and pursue what he really wanted to do in life.

While attending acting classes at Yale, Newman financially supported his family as a solicitor going door to door attempting to sell encyclopedias. Anyone who has ever engaged in direct sales know it's not an easy job. Most get doors slammed in their face if the homeowner even bothers to open the door at all. But this was not the case with Newman. He was surprisingly good in his efforts and was typically able to smooth talk his clients into giving him quite a few sales. The fact that he was incredibly handsome with charisma to spare certainly didn't hurt—especially when it came to his female clientele. He did so well, Newman would later recall, that at one point he made $900 in ten days. This was certainly a good paycheque in the 1950s.

Meanwhile at Yale, Paul's first break came when his directing professor—a fellow by the name of Frank McMullan— recruited him to play a part in an original production about the life of classical composer Ludwig van Beethoven. This then led to another breakthrough moment due to the fact of who was in the audience on opening night. Sitting in the crowd was a rather famous married couple in the theatrical business, William Liebling and Audrey Wood. Liebling worked as a kind of agent for acting talent and was impressed with Newman's performance—enough so, in fact, to chase after him backstage once it was all over. After introductions were made, he encouraged Newman to go to New York, where he could help him gain a higher status as a professional actor. Entertaining Liebling's suggestion, Paul decided to head to NYC as soon as he finished up his spring semester at Yale.

It was on this barest of leads that Newman and his fledgling family arrived in New York in the summer of 1951. Despite Liebling's praises and promises prior to his arrival, he didn't land Newman a major role immediately; instead, Newman had to scramble to find bit parts wherever he could. Yet it wasn't on the stage that he would find his next meal ticket, it was on the set of a television studio.

The early 1950s was the golden age of television, and TV producers were on the look for young, photogenic, and charismatic actors for the medium—Paul Newman fit this bill precisely. His television debut came when he managed to land a small part in *The March of Time*, which was a live, made-for-TV drama on the life of President McKinley. Newman was just an extra in this production, made into an elderly man through the magic of makeup, but this one simple appearance paid him an easy $75 on the spot and, more importantly, it would open the door for even more walk-on roles to come.

It was after Newman had built up his resume with these simple parts that he was able to shop around for larger parts. The first to come his way was a speaking role in the sci-fi themed TV show *Tales of Tomorrow*. Newman played the part of an army sergeant in a plot that centered around a natural disaster which had erupted when an enormous slab of ice had coalesced on America's western seaboard. After this role, he was then cast even more vigorously in TV shows such as *The Mask*, *The Web*, *You Are There*, and even an early TV soap opera called *The Aldrich Family*.

In the meantime, Newman was hearing more and more talk about New York's much-vaunted Actors Studio, where budding stars were seeking auditions. Newman himself would eventually get his own audition by accident. He had been asked by a female friend to fill in for a male co-star who had bailed on her just before her audition. Newman readily agreed to stand in as a replacement. The decision would prove to be fortuitous, because even though it was his friend who was supposed to be the main subject matter of the audition, Newman quickly stole the show. Those who saw his performance were so impressed that he was accepted into the prestigious enclave of the Actors Studio on the spot.

To his own shock and disbelief, by mere happenstance, Paul Newman had made it—and it was just about time considering the fact that his wife was now pregnant with their second child. Newman had a growing family to feed, and he hoped that the magic of the Actors Studio would help him be successful enough to meet their needs.

Chapter Four

Big Breaks and a Bad Bust

"I think he always thought of me as a lightweight. He treated me like he was disappointed in me a lot of the time, and he had every right to be. It has been one of the greatest agonies of my life that he could never know."

—Paul Newman, on his father

After several months of waiting, Newman's old mentor Liebling—the man who tempted him to come to New York in the first place—was able to finally make good on his promise to land Newman a part in a Broadway play. It was in 1953 that William Liebling received word that famed producer Joshua Logan was doing open auditions for a Broadway rendition of the William Inge production of *Picnic*. As soon as he heard of it, Liebling immediately thought of having Paul try out for a part. Initially, Newman aimed his sights for a smaller role in the production—that of a gas station clerk called Joker. It was a small part that consisted of a whopping one line, but it was at least enough to get his feet wet. By the time *Picnic* premiered, however, Newman had managed to charm his way into playing the much more significant role of Alan, the protagonist's friend.

Of further consequence with this production was the fact that it was on the set for *Picnic* that Newman met

Joanne Woodward. It was for Ms. Woodward that he would eventually leave his wife, and whom he would take as his second wife in 1958. But for the time being, during the production of *Picnic* in 1953, Paul Newman was all business and focused solely on perfecting his performance. His wife Jackie meanwhile gave birth to a healthy baby girl named Susan, and a third pregnancy resulting in her and Newman's final child together—Stephanie—would follow. It seemed that Newman's family grew just as his stardom did, and it was his stellar performance in *Picnic* that led to Newman to being awarded his first film contract in the form of the 1954 Warner Brothers feature *The Silver Chalice.*

In this film, Newman plays the role of a Greek slave from biblical times, who is commissioned by a Christian patriarch to fashion a receptacle for the silver chalice used during Christ's Last Supper. Although Newman tried his best, the film was ultimately viewed as a tremendous flop at the box office. Newman was mortified at the poor reception he received and immediately went into damage control to explain his dismal performance. Becoming an official apologist for the piece, he even put an ad in a publication explaining all the reasons why he felt the production went awry.

Nevertheless, Newman pushed on, and later that year, he showed up in a screen test alongside none other than James Dean, auditioning for a film called *East of Eden.* Newman ended up not making the cut for the part he auditioned for, while James Dean landed his role and made history for it. After failing to secure a part in *East of Eden*, Newman managed to get a part in another TV show—this time a lively musical with Frank Sinatra called *Our Town*. Written by the esteemed playwright Thornton Wilder, the color broadcast was a must-see event of the early television era.

Close on the heels of his work on *Our Town*, Newman was given a part in a TV adaptation of Ernest Hemingway's *The Battler*. Originally, he was cast in the role of Nick Adams, the passive chronicler who observes the main character, a boxer named Ad Francis. Once again crossing paths with James Dean, it was originally Dean that would play the title role. All of these plans fell through when on September 30, 1955, Dean was tragically killed in a car accident. As sad as the loss of the young, promising actor was, it was also a devastating hit to the film maker's bottom line.

It didn't take long, however, before the director began to look toward Paul Newman to take Dean's place. Newman at first declined out of respect for Dean, but after giving it some thought, he agreed to do it. Newman was then switched out of his initial role for another actor—Dewey Martin—and was himself used to fill in for Dean's part as Francis. Although the reviews for *The Battler* were decidedly mixed, it was this role that would serve as a springboard for further roles. One of them was the 1956 blockbuster *Somebody Up There Likes Me*, in which Newman portrayed the legendary boxer Rocky Graziano. The role of Rocky Graziano was yet another part that had been considered for James Dean, but again, due to his untimely demise, Paul Newman essentially became the runner up. Regardless of how Newman got the part, the production was a resounding success. Released around the

Fourth of July holiday, the piece received nothing but good reviews.

Elated by the results, on July 6, Newman took his wife to join some friends for a night on the town. Leaving their children with a babysitter in Long Island, the group met up at the Jolly Fisherman, a seafood joint in the nearby area of Roslyn. And the group of celebrants did indeed have a jolly good time—apparently a bit too jolly, in fact, because after hours a drunken Newman hopped into his car and went for a joy ride in which he clipped some shrubs at the Jolly Fisherman, slammed into a fire hydrant, and sped through a red light. It wasn't long before a squad car pulled him over. Incredibly enough, Newman didn't immediately pull to the side; instead, he led the police on a half-hearted chase for a mile or so before finally pulling to the side.

As daring as this move was, when the wary police officer who led the pursuit approached his driver's side window, Newman was not at all contrite. Instead, he growled at the policeman, "I'm acting for Rocky Graziano. What do you want?" Ironically enough, the approaching officer was a man by the name of Rocky Caggiano, and he readily informed the belligerent Newman, "I'm Rocky too, and you're under arrest!"

Chapter Five

Leaving His Wife

"People stay married because they want to, not because the doors are locked."

—Paul Newman

In the aftermath of his arrest, Newman began to do a lot of soul-searching. Although as his Kenyon days would attest, he never was one to shy away from a night of drunken revelry, he realized that there was something different about his desperate flight from police that night. Newman realized that there was a deep emotional unrest welling up inside of him that was threatening to spill out to the surface if it was not resolved. The source of the angst, he felt, was an ongoing affair that he had been carrying out with actress Joanne Woodward. Unbeknownst to his wife, Newman had been actively courting Woodward in between films, and their dalliances had become common knowledge among their peers scattered across various film sets. Newman was not yet ready to bring his betrayal out in the open, however, and kept shielding his wife from what others already knew.

In the midst of this turmoil, in the spring of 1957, Newman began work on a historical piece about Billy the Kid called *TheLeft Handed Gun*. Glad for a distraction, Newman threw himself into the role, attempting to keep his mind off of his own real-life drama. But by the time the summer months rolled around, he couldn't take it anymore and finally had a frank and candid discussion with his wife that resulted in him asking her for a divorce. Although she was devastated to hear of her husband's affair, Jackie, thinking of their children and how much harder her life would be without Newman, refused to let go so easily.

Much to Jackie's chagrin, by the time of Newman's next film *The Long, Hot Summer*, in which Joanne was his co-star, the two began to display their affection openly for the whole world to see. At last, unable to tolerate any further humiliation, Jackie agreed to work out the final terms of their divorce. Not wasting any time, Newman and Joanne then promptly got married on January 29, 1958 in Las Vegas. Paul Newman and Joanne Woodward have long been described as one of Hollywood's longest-lasting couples. It is true that the span of their marriage from 1958 until Newman's death in 2008 is indeed very long by Hollywood standards, but many often forget that one home had to be broken for this union to be created.

Shortly after leaving his wife and marrying Joanne Woodward, Newman moved into a new home on Manhattan's bustling 11th Street. For Newman, the more bohemian environment of Manhattan was a breath of fresh air when compared to the stifling and austere working-class neighborhood he had lived in with Jackie in Staten Island.

That year, Newman would star in the classic *Cat on a Hot Tin Roof*. His co-star for the piece, Elizabeth Taylor, would prove to have real-life drama of her own, however, when in the middle of production her husband Mike Todd suddenly died in a tragic plane accident. Amazingly, in the middle of her grief, Elizabeth Taylor was able to pull it together enough to finish her lines. The efforts proved to be worthwhile because *Cat on a Hot Tin Roof* would become one of the top ten rated films of 1958.

The following year, Paul and Joanne would make a special addition to their relationship with the arrival of their first child together, a healthy baby girl by the name of Elinor "Nell" Teresa. Paul Newman's next big film, meanwhile, was *Exodus*, in which he played an Israeli freedom fighter by the name of Ari Ben Canaan struggling to repatriate holocaust survivors to the Holy Land onboard a ship aptly named the *Exodus*. Despite some on-set difficulties, upon its release in 1960, the film would go on to become a box office hit, further cementing Newman's status as a top of the line movie star.

One of his most iconic roles would come shortly thereafter, when Newman was recruited to play the role of a pool shark by the name of Fast Eddie Felson in *The Hustler*. After Newman finished up his work on *The Hustler*, Joanne gave birth to Melissa, their second child, making Newman's large brood of dependents even bigger. Fortunately for them, proceeds from Newman's string of successful movies would provide more than enough money for the bills. *The Hustler* was also in the running for several awards, including best actor, best picture, and best screenplay.

At this point, Newman was appearing in approximately two major films a year. It took a lot of hard work and dedication, but neither Paul Newman nor his growing cadre of fans would expect anything less.

Chapter Six

Political Activism

"A man with no enemies is a man with no character."

—Paul Newman

Paul Newman was the kind of actor who almost always needed to study examples of the characters he played. And so, when he began shooting for the movie *Hud* in 1963, he was on location at a ranch in Claude, Texas, getting a feel for his character. The man he played was not a hero but rather an incorrigible roughneck by the name of Hud Bannon. Hud worked on a cattle ranch in the Texas Panhandle, and when he wasn't tending cattle, he was busy carousing with other men's wives and generally creating a disturbance. Hud Bannon was a bad guy who gave others a hard time, but Newman played him in such a way that he still managed to make the villain likable.

Newman would spend several weeks on location in Claude, Texas, and as such, he and the other cast members procured for themselves rooms at a hotel in nearby Amarillo. It didn't take long for the close-knit community to discover that a megastar was in their midst, and soon fans were swarming around the hotel in order to get a glimpse of Paul Newman. Most especially enthusiastic in this swarming were, of course, female fans wishing to meet the handsome heartthrob. Things got so bad that Paul would later recall, "Women were literally trying to climb through the transoms at the motel where I stayed."

Nevertheless, Paul managed to get through filming, and upon the movie's release, *Hud* would garner huge dividends at the box office in the spring of 1963. Later that summer, however, Newman took a brief break from the movie business to turn to an altogether different enterprise—civil rights activism. It was right around this time that Newman came into contact with civil rights leader Martin Luther King, Jr. and his Southern Christian Leadership Conference. Newman helped to recruit other star power to get a rally together in Los Angeles for a blockbuster event to raise money for the cause. Newman then followed this event with his participation in a sit-in protest right on the steps of California's state capitol building in Sacramento on June 12. The reason for the protest was to demand that action be taken over a failed fair housing bill.

Some people around Newman cautioned him about his outspoken stances, but he was adamant in his right to voice his views, or as he stated at the time, "Because I am a motion picture personality, I am not prepared to ignore what happens around me. Is it necessary or desirable to abdicate your responsibility as a citizen just because it might be safer for business? I cannot conveniently forget my responsibilities."

Newman would continue to support civil rights protests throughout the summer, leading up to Martin Luther King, Jr.'s famous march on Washington on August 28, 1963. Paul Newman would fondly recall the momentous event, "I'm proud I was there. There's never been anything like it." His early efforts in the civil rights movement in 1963 would prove to be a springboard for more vigorous political activism in 1964. It was during that election year that Newman worked with the Democratic National Convention to stump for Lyndon Johnson's presidential campaign. These efforts included a barbecue-fund raiser Newman helped to host in Long Island in honor of the president's daughter, Lynda Bird Johnson.

Shortly after this, in the fall of 1964, Newman went overseas to England to begin work on a comedy film called *Lady L* about a French woman who through her sheer force of will went from being a prostitute to a dame of a fine English estate—a feat that she is said to have accomplished through a wave of skullduggery. The entire feature would be shot at various locations between London, Paris, and Nice, and Newman decided to bring his family along for the ride.

Joanne was pregnant with what would be their final child together at the time, and in her delicate state, she was feeling a bit insecure in regard to Newman's beautiful co-star for the film, Sophia Loren. Nevertheless, Newman did everything he could to reassure his fretful wife that there was nothing but business between the two, and whenever asked about her, Newman would shrug off his interactions with her with bland platitudes such as, "Well, she was late for work this morning."

The film was a moderate success, but the success that Newman was more interested in was when that April, Joanne gave birth to a baby girl by the name of Claire Olivia. It seems that after wrapping up this film with Sophia Loren, Paul Newman had passed an important benchmark in his life with Joanne. He managed to prove to her that his family life with her was more important than any potential tryst with an attractive co-star like Sophia. With his dedication to the family reaffirmed, they could both breathe a mutual sigh of relief.

Chapter Seven

Life, Love, and Politics

"It's kind of like those little electric bumper cars where you drive around and see if you can hit the other guy. That's exactly what the country is like now. You no longer have the sense of community."

—Paul Newman

Rising high in the box office, in the fall of 1965, Newman was contacted by one of the greatest filmmakers of all time, Alfred Hitchcock. Hitchcock was working on a thriller piece called *Torn Curtain*, and he needed someone to play the role of an American scientist turned double agent hellbent on getting information from the communists to aid the United States. Newman was ready to pour himself into his work, but his efforts were interrupted when he became involved in a bad motorcycle accident.

The accident left him with bad burns and several skin grafts on his left hand, the latter of which would prove to be the most troubling. As Newman would later recall, "At first the doctors told me that I would never have the full use of my left hand again." The doctors then apparently recommended that Newman periodically grip a tennis ball in order to get his strength back. Newman had another idea: "I took a wet towel and wrung it all day. In the mornings my hands would have frozen and the towel would be as thick as a man's arm, but by the evening I would get it squeezed so dry that my fist was nearly locked tight." It was this routine that Newman used to get his hand back into working shape.

Due to his time spent in recovery, when Newman finally made his way to the set and took a look at the script, he found himself uneasy with how his part was shaping up. As filming commenced, Hitchcock would have his own share of disappointment as he began to consider that the actors he hired on for the production were just not conducive for what he had in mind. He proved to be correct in this estimation of events when the film was released. For all intents and purposes, *Torn Curtain* was a dud, with the *New York Times* declaring that it was "a pathetically undistinguished spy picture." Newman's next film, *Hombre*, which had him starring as John Russel in what was more or less a traditional western, didn't do that much better with some rather meager box office returns.

With such substandard fare, Paul Newman was beginning to wonder if his star was waning. Any such notion would soon be dispelled, however, when Newman took part in one of the most iconic films of all time, *Cool Hand Luke*. As was often the case in the roles that Newman reprised, for *Cool Hand Luke*, he went right down to the roots of the character he was to portray, paying a visit to rural West Virginia. Here he studied the locals, getting down how local guys talked, walked, and gesticulated.

Interestingly enough, Newman managed to get his brother a job on the set while shooting. Art Newman was recruited as a kind of unit manager, taking note of expenditures and making sure that the film stayed within its allotted budget. Those who saw Art on the set were startled at how much he looked like his brother Paul—albeit a "balding and more heavily built version." At any rate, the film stayed on budget and would go on to make a killing at the box office when it was finally released in November of 1967. More importantly for Newman, it proved that the then 42-year-old actor still had what it took to make a connection with an audience—and connect he did. Soon after the production, Paul was besieged by legions of fans. Much to his wife's chagrin, the middle-aged actor was widely regarded as a sex symbol, and young women would quite literally swoon in his presence.

It was around this time that Newman developed a rule of not giving autographs. As person after person held him up at this affair or that to get his signature (at one time even interrupting him at a urinal), he realized that the only way to avoid such nuisances was to make a solid ban on autographs altogether.

Still glowing from the success of *Cool Hand Luke*, Newman began the year 1968 on a high note. With some free time and a hefty payout from his box office success, he began to put his energy into other areas. One of those was the upcoming 1968 presidential election. Newman was a lifelong Democrat, and this election cycle he had one particular Democrat in mind—Senator Eugene McCarthy. Newman had already fallen away from Lyndon Johnson due to his stance on Vietnam, and in light of the Democratic president's decision not to seek re-election, Newman quickly proffered up McCarthy as his top pick in the now wide-open field. Soon he was appearing in TV ads and showing up at campaign stops to express his full support.

As he crisscrossed several states on the campaign trail, most of the time Newman was met with popular support. But this was not always the case. Of all his campaign stops, South Bend, Indiana would be the most negative experience he entertained because it was here that the campaign vehicle he and other members of the McCarthy team were riding in was intercepted by an angry crowd of opponents who began throwing rocks at them. In the end, Newman was frustrated to find that his efforts failed to gain any traction for McCarthy. Even worse, the other big contender that year, Bobby Kennedy, was gunned down by an assassin. This left the Democrats with Hubert Humphrey as their number one pick, but he would ultimately lose the general election to Richard Nixon.

Newman may have felt chastised by the turn of events, but no matter what happened in life, love, or politics, he wasn't willing to give up yet.

Chapter Eight

Butch Cassidy and the Sundance Kid

"Every time I get a script it's a matter of trying to know what I could do with it. I see colors, imagery. It has to have a smell. It's like falling in love. You can't give a reason why."

—Paul Newman

In the summer of 1968, Paul Newman was approached to do a film that seemed to fit his nature quite well. Called *Winning*, the film portrayed a group of race car drivers all jockeying for victory on the race track. With steely-eyed determination, these racers wanted to win on the track as much as Newman wanted to win in life. Newman played a rootless race car driver, who falls in love with a small-town divorcee, who in turn ends up betraying his trust for another driver. This drama is played out with the Indianapolis 500 as its background, demonstrating all the work the drivers put into the race in the months leading up to the Indy 500.

To get into this role, Newman went directly to Indiana to shadow Indianapolis 500 winners, such as Roger Ward and Bobby Unser, as he learned the IndyCar craft from them firsthand. Portraying the full scope of the Indy 500 proved problematic, however, and while the film was viewed as a good action piece, with plenty of insight into the race track, when it came to the personal dynamics and intrigue of the characters, it seemed to fall short. The film ultimately produced a mixed bag for movie-going audiences, and the reception of it was lukewarm.

Although *Winning* wasn't much of a winner at the box office, Newman's next film would be. In 1969, he was cast as Butch Cassidy in a portrayal of the classic western narrative *Butch Cassidy and the Sundance Kid*. It took a while to come up with just who would play his inevitable co-star—the Sundance Kid—until the role was ultimately given to an up-and-coming actor by the name of Steve McQueen. This selection would prove problematic when McQueen began to complain that he wasn't given top billing. Fed up, McQueen quit. The production team was then in a frantic search for a replacement.

It was Paul's wife Joanne who suggested Robert Redford. Redford, himself suspicious of the last-minute replacement, initially hesitated, but after some personal persuasion from Newman, he was finally convinced to sign onto the script. The film was finished in the fall of 1969 and received rave reviews. Its box office returns of more than $100 million bore testament to that fact, making it one of the biggest ticket sellers on record.

One of Newman's next big efforts after this was a production of Ken Kesey's *Sometimes a Great Notion*. This film depicted an Oregon family called the Stampers, who find themselves at odds with their logger neighbors who have joined a union and gone on strike. While everyone else refuses to work, the Stampers continue to slog it out.

Within this backdrop, the film follows the family dynamic of the Stampers and all of the problems therein. Newman began work on the film in the summer of 1970, but the final product would not be released until 1972, nearly two years later. The reviews were mixed, with some critics calling the film "muddled and bland." Nevertheless, this muddled and bland movie became the first attraction to be featured on the HBO cable network, airing on November 8, 1972.

It was that same year that Newman also began work on a decidedly different project—that of directing *The Effect of Gamma Rays on Man-in-the-Moon Marigolds* in which his wife would star. In this film, Joanne starred as Beatrice, a middle-aged woman upset with her lot in life. Yet another family-themed piece, the movie is centered around the world of Beatrice and her two daughters, as they seek to sort out their problems amongst each other. The film received descent reviews, and Joanne went on to win the acting prize at the Cannes Film festival.

Newman, meanwhile, had something else that was occupying his time in 1972—the re-election campaign of Richard Nixon. A decided Nixon opponent, Paul was determined to ensure that President Nixon did not get re-elected. Initially, he supported a Republican challenger to Nixon by the name of Pete McCloskey. But when McCloskey failed to gain traction, Newman began to support the eventual Democratic nominee, George McGovern.

Newman went on to be a participant at the 1972 Democratic "Together with McGovern" rally in Madison Square Garden. At this event, Newman was supposed to be an usher along with several other big-name stars, but when

Newman was rushed by fans in the audience, this would-be usher had to be ushered out by the police for his own protection. Besides attending rallies, Newman also starred in commercials for the DNC during the campaign. Just as was the case in 1968, these efforts fell flat, and instead of history recording the inauguration of a Democratic President McGovern, Nixon handily won re-election. President Nixon, of course, would be forced to resign in the middle of his second term due to the Watergate scandal, but it was little solace to Newman who was left routinely frustrated over his political bets.

Chapter Nine

Late Life and the Death of His Son

"I've been accused of being aloof. I'm not. I'm just wary."

—Paul Newman

By the mid-1970s, despite a few duds, Paul Newman was absolute Hollywood royalty. Like any potentate, he wished to extend his legacy to his children, and in particular to his only son Scott. An opportunity for this passing of the torch came in 1974 with the production of the film *The Towering Inferno*. While Paul starred in one of the lead roles, Scott was given a smaller role as a firefighter. Even though some lambasted the movie as being focused more on special effects than quality acting, the action-packed thriller was ultimately a success and garnered big returns at the box office. Much of this money, Newman would come to invest in a burgeoning racing career.

By the mid-1970s, Newman, who officially competed under the name of P.L. Newman, was a regular face on the race track—regular enough to end up in a series of bad wrecks, at least one of which could have taken his life. The incident occurred at a race track in Lime Rock Park in Connecticut, when the car he was driving failed to brake properly. Unable to stop, the actor was forced to steer his car down an escape path that allowed him to exit the track. After barreling through the escape path, he still wasn't quite able to stop and instead rolled his car around so that the left side slammed into a group of trees, bringing his out-of-control ride to a violent end.

Onlookers who rushed to the scene saw the left side of the car completed caved in and thought that Newman had been killed, but once Newman stepped out of the vehicle, they realized that his car had the steering wheel on the right side. It was indeed a controlled crash, and Newman had purposefully sent his left side into the trees to shield himself from the brunt of the collision.

When he wasn't investing his time and money in the racing, Newman was filming his next feature, a movie that had him cast as an abrasive hockey coach named Reggie Dunlop. The film was called *Slap Shot* and was released in 1977 with returns of over $28 million at the box office. This was a good number to be sure, but it was absolutely dwarfed by the other blockbusters that came out that summer, such as *Star Wars*, *Close Encounters of the Third Kind*, and *Smokey and the Bandit*.

Newman's next film, the post-apocalyptic *Quintet* would be a complete and unequivocal box office bomb. This would prove to be the least of Newman's worries, however, because his son Scott would die of a drug overdose in late 1978. Shortly after appearing in the 1977 film *Fraternity Row*, Scott succumbed to substance abuse. In 1978, his family had tried to stage an intervention, getting him to briefly see an addiction counsellor, but sadly it was all to no avail. Scott had begun a drug and alcohol binge on November 19—taking Valium and other drugs interspersed with liberal amounts of alcohol—that ended with him dying in his sleep in the early morning hours of November 20, 1978.

Paul Newman was understandably shocked and deeply grieved by his son's death, yet at the same time, he and many in the family couldn't help but see it coming. They knew that Scott was in dangerous territory; they just didn't know how to get him out of it. Once this tragic juncture was reached, Newman sought to educate the public about drug abuse so that other families could avoid suffering the same fate. It was these efforts that would eventually crystallize in the establishment of the Scott Newman Center.

With the passing of his son, it was hard for Newman to get back on track, but he eventually managed to craft another box office success in the form of *Fort Apache, The Bronx*. Newman played a rugged police detective in this crime drama, stationed in New York's 41st precinct, which was so rough at the time that the police had nicknamed it Fort Apache. Shooting for the feature began in March of 1980 but was almost immediately beset with problems. After community leaders read the script, they were incensed at what they viewed as a poor depiction of the Bronx. Eventually, the protests grew loud enough that the script was modified to make mention of the honest citizens of the neighborhood to make clear that not everyone who lived around Fort Apache was a criminal.

Despite these efforts, by the time the film came out in February, the movie seemed like a damaged product and failed to pay the dividends that its creators had hoped. Fortunately for Newman, he would end up completely vindicated in his next film when he starred in *Absence of Malice* in 1981. The film takes an attack on journalistic malfeasance, something that Newman could relate to in light of all the tabloid journalism that surrounded his family in the aftermath of his son's death.

In the meantime, in the early 1980s, Newman once again delved into politics, going on record in the public arena to voice strong criticism of then-President Ronald Reagan's policies. Newman often found the Republican president to be recklessly aggressive in his saber-rattling challenges to the Soviet Union. In Newman's criticism of Reagan, he provoked an unexpected combatant in the form of Charlton Heston. Heston began to appear in public forums rebutting many of Newman's critiques and arguments. As the feud between the two celebrities grew, they were eventually invited to openly debate each other on the late-night talk show *The Last Word*.

Shying away from politics shortly after this exchange, Newman would embark on something completely different. Right around this time, he would form his own food company called Newman's Own. He started out by creating his own brands of salad dressing, then eventually his own pasta sauce, popcorn, lemonade, and other favorites. The food was good, but what made it special was the fact that Newman didn't profit from their sales; instead, he made sure that the money procured from his products was sent directly to charity. This has resulted in hundreds of millions of dollars being sent to charities in Paul Newman's name. This, along with a return to his passion of race cars, would take up much of Newman's time during the mid-1980s.

It wasn't until the 1986 smash hit *The Colour of Money* that Newman would get back on track when it came to movies. In this movie, he reprised his old *Hustler* role of Fast Eddie, except this time Eddie's all grown up and working alongside a younger protégé played by Tom Cruise. The movie was a sensation both in and outside of the theater and would net some $50 million in ticket sales. Newman also managed to win an Oscar for his role, a feat that had evaded him until this point in his career. After this success, Newman would go on to star in many more films such as *Blaze, Mr. & Mrs. Badge*, and *Message in a Bottle*. The latter of which again paired the old actor with a younger star—this time Kevin Costner—in the hopes that the dynamic would pay off. When the film was released in February of 1999, most of the reviews were negative but it still managed to do well in the box office, grossing $118 million.

Arguably one of Newman's most memorable appearances of this time period was not in a feature film but on an episode of *The Simpsons*. After an absurd sequence of events, the character Marge Simpson tells her husband Homer that she has a crush on the cartoon lumberjack whose image is emblazoned on a package of paper towels. Homer then goes to sleep and dreams of another iconic animated advert. He dreams about a bottle of Newman's Own salad dressing, in which Newman's painted-on face comes to life. In regard to being Homer's crush, Paul Newman's voice can then be heard, telling the misguided Homer, "Homer, I'll tell you what I told Redford. It ain't gonna happen."

Conclusion

At the dawn of the new millennium, Newman wasn't necessarily looking for the next major blockbuster, but when he began shooting in the spring of 2001 for the now cult-favorite *Road to Perdition*, he would soon realize that he had a box office hit on his hands. Starring alongside Tom Hanks, the film is a historic piece that takes us into the world of a midwestern crime syndicate operating in the 1930s. Fittingly enough, the film was shot in Chicago, where it absorbed all the urban legacy of the city's gangster past. *Road to Perdition* debuted in movie theatres in the summer of 2002 and managed to bring in some $180 million.

It was a couple of years after wrapping up this film that Newman embarked upon what would be his last major production project, starring as the elder patriarch Max Roby in the dramatic mini-series entitled *Empire Falls*. For his role in *Empire Falls*, Paul Newman would receive both a Primetime Emmy and a Golden Globe in 2006. But perhaps his most iconic role of all in his later years would be that of Doc Hudson, an old race car in the Pixar computer-animated movie *Cars*.

Shortly after this performance, it became apparent that the hitherto fast life of Paul Newman was beginning to slow down. Many felt that Paul was getting ready to retire from the business altogether. Then in 2007, during an appearance he made for *Good Morning America*, Paul Newman answered this question for good by remarking unequivocally, "I'm not able to work anymore as an actor at the level I would want to. You start to lose your memory, your confidence, your invention. So that's pretty much a closed book for me. I've been doing it for fifty years. That's enough."

So that was it, after several decades of nonstop film and television roles, Newman announced that he was going to hang up his hat for good. Sadly, it was shortly after this announcement was made that his health began a sharp decline. His next birthday came on January 26, 2008; he was 83 years old, and he was finally beginning to show it. There had been rumors that he had been struggling with cancer and even reports of him visiting the waiting rooms of oncologists, looking skinny and weak as he waited to be seen. One of his last public appearances seemed to verify these earlier reports when Newman appeared at the Indy 500 in May of 2008 looking very thin indeed.

Newman, when speaking to the press that day, left everyone with the haunting refrain, "One thing we're looking forward to is winning this race. There are other races, and God knows eight championships is nothing to be sneezed at, but we'll be there one of these days. I may be someplace else watching from above, but we're going to win this one way or the other."

Although he had tried to keep it quiet, Paul Newman had been battling an aggressive form of lung cancer for months. As Paul always did, he struggled to overcome his adversity, but in the end, even he was forced to momentarily concede defeat, and he passed out of this world on September 26, 2008.